G000123305

the most common objection to belief in God. If God is both good and all-powerful, then surely evil and suffering would not exist. The world is characterised by violence, pain and suffering, so God – if he exists – either lacks goodness or has limited power.

The problem of pain

You might ask: "If God is meant to be good and all-powerful, how can he allow my parents' marriage to fall apart, or simply stand by while my father dies painfully on a hospital bed?" On a much bigger scale, what about those nightmare images of starving children and earthquake victims?

Surely, an all-knowing God would have known that evil would come into his world and an all-powerful God would be able to stop it and a good God would want to prevent evil in the first place. Evil clearly exists, which surely confirms the atheistic objection and makes it a serious challenge to belief in God.

Atheism or theism?

"I cannot imagine any omnipotent sentient being sufficiently cruel to create the world we inhabit" (Iris Murdoch, *A Severed Head*); **"The only excuse for God is that he doesn't exist"** (Stendhal, the French sceptic).

We must start with the most basic of choices of belief or unbelief: atheism or theism.

God either exists or he doesn't. If God doesn't exist, then we should expect the atheistic explanations about our suffering to be more satisfying than the theistic one. It ought to tune in intuitively with our experience of living in a godless universe. If atheism is to be reliable and useful in thinking about suffering, we have a right to demand that it offers more substantial and convincing answers than anything Christianity can offer. So let's ask our heartfelt questions within an atheistic framework.

A blind pitiless universe

Why did the Haiti earthquake happen, killing so many children and innocent people? Why did an earthquake and tsunami hit Japan? Why is life characterised by so much heartache? Atheism replies: "You can't ask a cold, random and impersonal universe the question 'why?' Every part of our existence is merely the fallout of a random, chance explosion at the birth of the universe. It is a nonsense question. So just pull yourself together and be a survivor."

Richard Dawkins answers in this way: **"The universe we observe has precisely the properties we should expect if there is, at bottom, no design, no purpose, no evil and no good, nothing but blind pitiless indifference."**[1] The universe is cold, blind, silent and pitilessly indifferent to our suffering. This

atheistic view is echoed by Francis Crick, the DNA-discovering Nobel prize-winning scientist: **"You, your joys and your sorrows, your memories and your ambitions, your sense of personal identity and free will, are in fact no more than the behaviour of a vast assembly of nerve cells and their associated molecules."**[2] Christopher Hitchens, a prominent atheist who tragically is dying of throat cancer, said: **"To the dumb question 'Why me?' the cosmos barely bothers to return the reply: Why not?"**[3]

Are you satisfied with answers that deny your most basic and primal intuition that suffering is not how things should be? The joy of having a child and the sorrow of losing one must be more than the behaviour of a vast assembly of nerve cells and their associated molecules? Surely it is our basic intuitions about the world and how it ought to be that cause us to ask these agonising "Why?" questions. Such intuitions prompt us to cry out in the middle of our suffering for answers, for fresh perspective and

renewed strength to keep going. Where does such intuition come from? Is it merely a cosmic prank, an evolutionary sick joke? Atheism dismisses such intuition along with our agonising "Why?" questions, for in a godless universe, there is no one there to see your anger or hear your questions. Atheism, like Buddhism, remains calm and serene in the face of suffering and removes itself from any critique or outrage.

What does atheism offer in the face of suffering?

In the immediate aftermath of tsunamis, earthquakes and terrorist attacks, the otherwise ubiquitous media atheists seem to become somewhat invisible. At such times atheism's voice sounds shrill and hollow, because atheism lacks the categories to speak into suffering with words of understanding, comfort, motivation and hope.

Should we not be concerned that atheism dismisses our intuitions about who we are and the way the world should be? Atheism regards such self-awareness as an inexplicable evolutionary malfunction, a genetic discrepancy.

The suffering question assumes the existence of God

Perhaps the main reason we find suffering to be such a moral problem is because deep down we think of this world as belonging to a good all-powerful God, so that when something terrible or unfair does happen, we are easily outraged that God should permit such a thing.

If we remove God from the equation, we still have to endure suffering, but not the agonising problem of "Why?" Suffering just is! The human story without God is no more than a survival of the fittest. So, far from disproving God, our "Why suffering?" questions assume his existence.

Thoughtful writers such as Sheldon Vanauken and C S Lewis (both of whom watched their wives die slow, painful deaths) have suggested that suffering brings our intuitive belief in God to the surface, like a wake-up call.

"God whispers to us in our pleasures, speaks in our conscience, but shouts in our pains; it is his megaphone to rouse a deaf world."[4]

What is God like?

So we need to move on from asking, "How could a good, all-powerful God let suffering happen?" and "Does God exist?" to "What is God like?" God's existence is assumed in the "Why suffering?" question. It is his character that is being disputed. That's the real problem posed by suffering. What is God like? Does he even care? Isn't he meant to be all-powerful and good? If so, then how is it possible to have so much suffering in the world?

"Is he [God] willing to prevent evil, but not able? Then he is impotent. Is he able but not willing? Then he is malevolent. Is he both able and willing? Whence then is evil?" (Epicurus).

Either God has lost the plot or he is spiteful since he seems perfectly content to allow suffering which he is able to prevent. That's probably the simplest way for Christians to answer the problem: either to limit God in his power or suggest he is serene and morally neutral about suffering.

Dualism

Let's consider the first option, which theologians call "dualism" – we might call it good versus evil or God versus Satan. Instead of God being all-powerful, he is working against an equally powerful and malignant force. God remains good and is fully occupied fighting the dark side, which at times seems at least as powerful. In this view we are effectively letting God off the hook by blaming bad stuff on the devil, who provokes people to hijack planes and causes sickness and earthquakes, tsunamis and train derailments. Meanwhile a good, but limited, God is rushing around trying to put out the fires and make everything right.

Good things from God and bad things from the devil?

On the surface, it does seem to make sense, but according to the Bible it's not that simple: **"I form the light and create darkness, I bring prosperity and create disaster; I, the LORD, do all these things"** (Isaiah 45:7, NIV). The God of the Bible is sovereign in his running of the universe and nothing happens outside his control. Satan is an agent of evil, but is only finite and not a near equal. He is only able to operate within the world (until his ultimate judgement) because God permits him to.

Besides, if there were a duality in the universe, then God's purposes might ultimately be thwarted. It wouldn't matter how noble God's character and aspirations were if he was incapable of bringing things under his Icontrol. Christians, in rejecting dualism, have confidence that one day God will end the evil, injustice and violence of this world, and that righteousness will cover the earth as the waters cover the sea.

Monism

The other possible move is to blur the categories of good and evil and conclude that because God brings about light and darkness, maybe God has a dark side to him. In this view, the problem with suffering is simply one of perspective. If we were truly enlightened we would perceive everything to be one, rather than divided into the dualities of good and evil, suffering and pleasure, kindness and cruelty. What we call good and evil, light and darkness are not to be opposed to one another but blended into an undifferentiated oneness.

This, like dualism, would solve our problem with evil and suffering by changing our view of both God and suffering. The Bible's revelation of God's character, seen most clearly in Jesus, will not allow this (largely Buddhist) view to prevail.

If we have to reject dualism to be sure there is a heaven to inherit, then we must also reject monism to be sure there is a heaven worth inheriting. One reason God hates suffering in his world is that it is closely linked to human rebellion and wickedness. It is because God hates evil and suffering that we can be assured heaven is a place where such things will be no more.

"God is light; in him there is no darkness at all" (1 John 1:5, NIV). God is good, loving, righteous and just. There is no alter ego or dark side to him. God did not create evil; he simply made human beings with the capacity to reject him and so contract an evil nature themselves. It's because God goes on record as not approving of suffering and evil and of being committed to eradicating them that we can have confidence in his character that he is not a mixture of good and evil. God does not remain unmoved in the face of suffering. Jesus spent a large proportion of his time healing the sick, because it was God's will to alleviate the consequences of a fallen and rebellious world. The desire to reflect God's character has led the Christian church to be at the forefront of alleviating poverty, educating the ignorant, contending for justice, opposing corruption and healing the sick all around the world.

Squaring the circle

Having rejected two false moves which would strip God of his attributes of power or goodness, Christianity is left open to two profound objections: if God hates evil and suffering so much why does he put up with it? And why do innocents suffer?

In some way God sees it necessary to the moral order of his universe to permit a certain amount of suffering in his world as a penalty for human rebellion and wickedness. We humans would be blissfully unaware that we have provoked God's righteous anger if there were never any consequences for our behaviour. If the toast always landed butter side up , and there were no painful consequences for our actions, we would be living in a fool's paradise.

Therefore, it is hard to escape the uncomfortable and difficult conclusion that God (for some undisclosed reasons) allows things to go on in his world to which he is thoroughly opposed. That seems to be a conclusion the Bible pushes us towards.

An indecent proposal

The shocking suggestion of God imposing a penalty on the world leaves itself open to the misunderstanding that all suffering is a direct consequence of God's judgement. Not so, according to the Bible; rather, there are two basic types of suffering.

As a young boy, I managed to set my parents' garage on fire by lighting fireworks inside it and then walking away. Following hard on the heels of my pyrotechnic show, which ultimately gathered the entire neighbourhood, was the sudden realisation that my actions had consequences. I was to experience both intrinsic and imposed suffering as a result of my firework stunt. *Intrinsic* to my actions was the conflagration of all my toys stored in the garage. Second was the swift and memorable punishment *imposed* on me by my parents!

Intrinsic suffering

Suffering that is intrinsic to our actions accounts for the vast proportion of misery in the world. Operating an economic system that does not pay a fair wage to developing world farmers and allows 300,000 people to die needlessly every week from starvation is down to human greed and complacency. Similarly, governments and corporations which do not use adequate materials when building schools and houses in an earthquake zone (as in Haiti) are usually only thinking about maximising profit.

Most writers on the subject seem to agree that most suffering in this world is caused directly by humanity: war; oppression of individuals and groups; starvation arising from war and corruption; illness caused by pollution of the environment. Though these things are terrible, they are consistent with the Christian analysis of the human fallen condition. They are self-inflicted wounds.

Imposed suffering

Though the largest proportion of human suffering is attributable to deliberate and reckless behaviour towards our planet and fellow creatures, nevertheless an irreducible amount of misery remains that cannot be so easily laid at our door. Natural disasters such as earthquakes and resulting tsunamis are often cited as arguments against the existence of a loving God, along with other misfortunes such as sickness and genetic abnormalities which appear to strike indiscriminately without any obvious human cause.

The Bible's explanation is that this world and our stewardship of it has fallen from an original perfection. Our rebellion against God had grave consequences for the world. The first consequence of being alienated from God was that humans became diminished in their desire for, and capacity to, look after the natural environment and for one another. In that original God-intended state, one can imagine humans who would have been more in tune with the natural environment and would, like certain other mammals, have been able to detect (for example) an approaching tsunami. They would have had similar instincts for volcanic activity and would have been wise enough to avoid building vulnerable houses on a fault line. What was once a harmless and exciting display of God's creative power is now a source of dread and destruction.

Furthermore, God wanted to register his disapproval and provide a reminder of the consequences of human rebellion. He did this by altering the conditions in which humans lived. Rather than living in a perfect garden, humans were cast into a fallen and wild earth, still mind-numbingly beautiful, but much more hostile and harder to look after than it would have been. We became vulnerable to the diseases and decay that emerged from a poorly-stewarded world.

It seems God felt it necessary to impose a level of punishment and disapproval on humanity so that we would recognise the nature of the world we are living in and live accordingly. Sadly, we have not responded well and rather than work together to live wisely in a fallen world (eg drain all malarial swamps and make universal vaccinations cheaply available for all), we have continued to rebel against God and his ways and values.

Why doesn't God **stop all** the suffering?

So far, we have considered two choices (theism or atheism) and rejected two false views of God (dualism and monism). We have also reflected on the two basic types of suffering, intrinsic and imposed.

We are still left with two main objections. **Why doesn't God stop all the suffering?** And **why do innocents suffer?** The big objection to suffering is that it violates our view of what we think life should be like. So, how should we expect God to stop suffering without similarly violating our humanity? If a drunk driver was about to kill a child, how should a loving, powerful God intervene without robbing us of our responsibility? Should God lift the child out of the way of the car or lift the car over the child? In such a world we would not be properly human if we were unable to choose and take responsibility for our actions. We would be more like puppets whose strings are pulled to protect us from any possible harm. Even the most obsessive parents know that unless their children are eventually allowed to take responsibility for their actions they will not become mature adults.

Another way of reducing suffering would be for God to remove all the evil people from the world. You might understandably have murderers at the top of your list for removal, but where does God finish if he is to prevent human greed and pride resulting in further misery? Should he remove you and me before we cause suffering in our families, friendships or marriage? That's the tricky bit: where does God stop and who sets the standard? Should there be any mitigating circumstances for those from poor and dysfunctional backgrounds in which crime is more endemic? Surely the only fair mechanism is a final judgement in which God impartially judges all people for the suffering and evil they have personally caused in his world.

Why innocents?

With regard to why some people suffer rather than others, the Bible refuses to blame individuals. The long-suffering Job was accused by his religious friends of having incurred God's anger. Similarly, in John's Gospel, a man born blind was thought to be suffering for either his or his parents' sinful actions. On both occasions the answer comes loud and clear. What do we really know? This is not a judgement on people but is linked to a much more complex and profound mystery that lies at the heart of reality (see Job chapters 38 to 42 and John chapter 9).

Why can't God organise it so that calamity always comes to people in precise proportion to their sins? One answer the Bible gives is that it is not possible for suffering to work that way because we are human. We are social creatures who possess a unique kind of solidarity: one person's actions potentially affects millions. Whether a rogue trader who destroys pension funds or a terrorist who poisons the air conditioning in a major subway, the human race suffers together in a painful but unavoidable solidarity.

In one man we are all guilty

In the Bible, the apostle Paul says the "whole human race is guilty in Adam" (Romans 3:9-19; 5:12,19). The choices Adam made to disobey God represented the choices we would have made if we were in his situation. This shows there is a collective dimension to sin itself. *Since we all share a common sinfulness, we shouldn't be surprised that we also share a common suffering.* This is why "innocents" suffer: the actions and neglect of all people in all places and all time are linked and cascade down through relationships, social structures and the physical fabric of this world.

We can't therefore avoid being collectively involved in one another's sins and the suffering they cause; whether it be suffering that is intrinsic to those sinful actions or suffering which is tied into those conditions God has imposed

on this world in response to our
rebellion.

Two choices

This brings us full circle: we are faced
with two alternative interpretations of
things:

1   Reality is chaotic and meaningless.
    Events we call good are just chance
    happenings thrown up by the laws of
    statistics, and events we call bad must
    have an equal moral value of "neutral".
    On this atheistic world view, there are no
    ultimate values of good, bad or evil. Or:

2   As we enjoy the good and beautiful
    aspects of life, we can think that is the
    way things should really be, and that evil
    and suffering are a result of some
    distortion that has crept into a
    fundamentally good world. This is the
    Bible's view.

The best fit

Although unanswered questions still remain, at a fundamental level the Bible's view of evil and suffering makes more sense, of who we are and how we respond to suffering, than atheism does. The Bible points us away from the glib, simplistic answers offered by atheism, dualism or monism. It even points us away from the ambiguities of our world to an even more startling paradox.

An innocent man hanging on a cross

The greatest confirmation of God's love for suffering humanity is the anguished figure of one suffering man. God entered the genetic solidarity of the human race from birth to death in the form of Jesus of Nazareth. Jesus uniquely stood as both our representative and God's. The only truly innocent person who ever lived willingly laid down his life and took upon himself the curse and brokenness that human rebellion brought into the world.

Just as death came through one man, the ultimate end to death and suffering will come from the death and resurrection of this one man.

As a man, Jesus stands in solidarity with us, fully representing the human race, but he also and uniquely represents God. By his death on the cross God incarnate satisfied God's own just demands for human wickedness to be punished. In so doing, Jesus has paved the way for a new world order to be formed at the end of time, one in which there will be no more suffering, tears or death. This is only possible because the root cause of all suffering and evil has been dealt with in Jesus' death and resurrection. Jesus achieved all this, not by remaining serene and detached from our pain, but through his own suffering, tears and death.

The death of Christ mirrors all those questions we have asked of suffering:

Was Jesus' death due to God's lack of power or moral goodness?

Why did Jesus experience further suffering imposed by God?

Why did the innocent Jesus suffer while evildoers escape punishment?

Can we seriously believe it was God's will that people should crucify his Son? The answer is both yes and no. It was not God's will, in that he did not approve of the jealousy, pride and murderous conspiracy that took Jesus to the cross.

But it was God's will in that he permitted Jesus' death as part of his bigger plan to put an end to evil and suffering by taking the human penalty for sin upon himself.

Why didn't God put a stop to Jesus' suffering? It was because of God's love for you and for me. God allowed Jesus to lay down his life so that we could have our friendship with God restored and experience peace, strength and comfort in our present suffering, with the certain knowledge that evil and suffering will one day be wiped from God's creation.

God knows about suffering. He watched his own Son being tortured and murdered and he could have stopped it, but he didn't because it was the only means by which we could be forgiven and evil and suffering could be dealt with justly.

So what?

During Christmas week in 2007 my eleven-year-old nephew was told by a hospital consultant that he was going to die. A scan had just revealed the sudden and aggressive spread of multiple brain and spine tumours.

David, my sister's son, looked into the doctor's eyes and said: "I'm not afraid of dying, doctor – I have a friend called Jesus who will take me to be with him for ever."

The doctor smiled warmly and said, "David, I'm so glad you know Jesus for he is my friend and Saviour also."

David continued to trust God until he died just ten weeks later, in the certain knowledge that Jesus had defeated death and provided the means by which he would one day be given a new body and would live in a new world without suffering, sickness, tears and death.

Whether you were brought up in a Christian home like David or whether you were brought up as a Buddhist, like his hospital consultant, you too can be given the same comfort and confidence in the face of suffering and death.

Your response

If you would like to investigate further the key evidence for Christianity visit www.bethinking.org/booklets and choose from a variety of talks and articles.

If you are ready to make the step of asking God to be at the centre of your life as your Lord then he is only a prayer away:

Prayer

"

Lord God,

I acknowledge that you care far more about the suffering of this world than I could ever imagine.

I admit that I have lived independently of you and have offended your love and provoked your anger with my proud, selfish attitude to you and all that you have made.

I thank you that in Jesus you took on human form and broke into history as a man. I thank you that Jesus Christ was not exempt from suffering.

I accept that it was only in Jesus that human sin and rebellion were dealt with and punished. Thank you that Jesus willingly laid down his life for me, bearing the punishment my sin deserves and offering me the forgiveness I don't deserve.

I now turn away from everything that is wrong in my life and ask you to forgive me by virtue of who Jesus is and what he achieved on the cross.

Please send the Spirit of Jesus to live in me, to renew me and help me to be a follower of Jesus from this day on and for the rest of my life.

Amen.

If you have prayed this prayer, speak to a Christian friend or go to our website www.bethinking.org/booklets and email us using "Contact us".

Footnotes

1   Richard Dawkins, *River out of Eden: A Darwinian View of Life* (London: Weidenfeld and Nicolson, 1995, page 133).).

2   Francis Crick, *The Astonishing Hypothesis: The scientific search for the Soul* (New York: Charles Scribner's Sons, 1994, page 3.).

3   http://www.vanityfair.com/culture/features/2010/09/hitchens-201009. Accessed on 31 March 2011.

4   C S Lewis, *The Problem of Pain* (New York: Macmillan, 1962, page 93).